Looking at Small Mammals

Marsupials

Sally Morgan

Chrysalis Children's Books

First published in the UK in 2004 by
Chrysalis Children's Books
An imprint of Chrysalis Books Group Plc
The Chrysalis Building, Bramley Road
London W10 6SP

Editorial manager: Joyce Bentley
Series editor: Debbie Foy
Editors: Clare Lewis, Joseph Fullman
Designer: Wladek Szechter
Picture researcher: Sally Morgan
Illustrations: Woody

ISBN 1 84458 103 9

Printed in China

10 9 8 7 6 5 4 3 2 1

British Library Cataloguing in Publication Data for this
book is available from the British Library.

Picture acknowledgements:
Ecoscene: 14, 21B Edward Bent; 12 John Farmer; 27B
Michael Gore; 5T, 32 Simon Grove; 4 Alexandra
Elliott Jones; 3, 6, 9T, 11T, 13T, 16, 17T, 19B, 21T, 26,
27T Wayne Lawler; 1, 5B, 7B, 9B, 15T Michael
Maconachie; 7T Robert Pickett; 25T & B Kjell
Sandved; 10, 17B, 18 Alan Towse. Front cover: B &
TCL Wayne Lawler; TR Robert Picket; TL, CL & CR
Michael Maconachie; TCR Alan Towse. Back cover:
TCL Wayne Lawler; TR Robert Pickett; TL Michael
Maconachie; TCR Alan Towse. Corbis: 13B Joe
McDonald; 22 & 23B Martin Harvey; 23T Eric and
David Hosking. NHPA: 20 Bruce Beehler. Still
Pictures: 2, 15B, 24 John Cancalosi; 19T Alain
Compost; 11B Gunter Ziesler.

Contents

Introducing marsupials

Marsupials belong to a group of animals called **mammals.** Most mammals have four legs and are covered in hair. They give birth to live young.

Koalas spend most of their time in trees.

Young mammals feed on their mother's milk for the first months of their lives. There are many different types of marsupials. They vary in colour, size and the food they eat. The koala and wombat are examples of marsupials.

The pademelon is a shy marsupial that lives in the rainforests of Australia. It comes out to feed at night.

5

What are marsupials?

All marsupials have a **pouch**. The pouch is a fold of skin or pocket in which they keep their young.

This wallaby has a youngster in its large pouch.

The kowari is a small marsupial with a squirrel-like head and a long tail. It lives in burrows.

The young feed on their mother's milk while they are safely hidden inside their mother's pouch. There are about 250 different types of marsupials. The smallest of all the marsupials is the tiny dasyure and the largest marsupial is the kangaroo.

The koala gives birth to one baby. It stays in her pouch for six months and then it is carried on her back.

Where do marsupials live?

Marsupials are only found in certain parts of the world. Most marsupials live in Australia but they are also found in New Zealand and parts of North and South America.

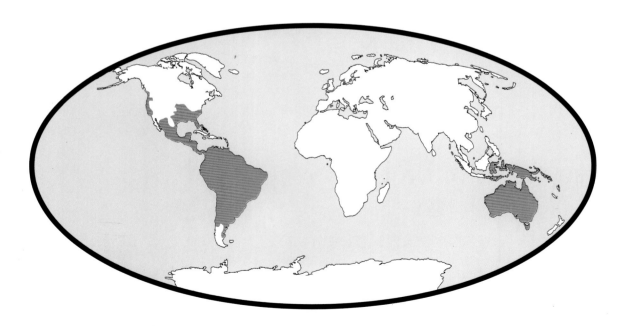

The areas shaded in pink on this map of the world show where marsupials live.

Agile wallabies live in Australia and New Guinea, where they are found in grasslands and forests.

Koalas are found in eucalyptus trees in Australia.

Marsupials live on land. They can be found in forests, mountains, grasslands and in parks and gardens. Some can even survive in deserts.

Plant eaters

Some marsupials eat nothing but plants. They are called **herbivores**. The koala bear is a particularly fussy eater as it only eats leaves from gum trees.

A koala carefully chooses a leaf, bites it off and grinds it up with its teeth before swallowing it.

The bettong feeds on leaves, seeds, flowers and roots.

Possums eat leaves, fruits and bark. The honey possum is the size of a mouse and has a long tail. It also has a long tongue, which can reach right into flowers to sip the **nectar** and lick up pollen.

The honey possum comes out at night to feed on the pollen and nectar of flowers.

Meat eaters

Many marsupials are **carnivores.** This means they eat other animals. Carnivorous marsupials have sharp teeth to catch and hold their **prey** and then to eat them!

The sharp teeth and powerful jaws of the Tasmanian devil are used to tear skin and crush bone.

*The antechinus,
a type of dasyure,
is an insect-eating
marsupial.*

They eat animals such as lizards, birds, small mammals and insects. The largest carnivores include the Tasmanian devil and the quoll.

*The Virginia opossum
feeds on insects, mice
and rabbits. Sometimes
it will even kill chickens.*

13

Seeing and smelling

Marsupials learn about their surroundings by using their senses. Many marsupials are **nocturnal**. This means they hunt at night.

Sugar gliders leap from tree to tree. They have eyes that point forwards to help them judge the distance between trees.

The koala has small round eyes and a large black nose.

Night hunters have large eyes to help them see in the dark. Many marsupials rely on their sense of smell to find their way and to locate food. The numbat uses smell to find its favourite food, termites. Bandicoots use smell to find spiders or worms in the soil.

The numbat uses its sense of smell and hearing to find termites, its favourite food.

Getting around

Marsupials move around in different ways.

Some hop and jump while others waddle

slowly along the ground.

The agile wallaby hops along the ground using its long back legs and its tail for balance.

The rufous bettong spends its daytime in a nest and emerges at night to feed.

Some marsupials, such as wallabies and potoroos, have extra long back legs for jumping and hopping. Their long tail helps them to balance.

The wombat is a heavy animal with short, powerful legs. Although it runs slowly, it can travel long distances each night.

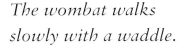
The wombat walks slowly with a waddle.

Living in trees

Many marsupials live in trees and are expert climbers. They have feet with long claws so they can get a good grip on the tree trunk. A few marsupials have a tail that can grip branches.

Koalas climb by gripping the tree trunk with the claws of their front feet and bringing up their hind feet.

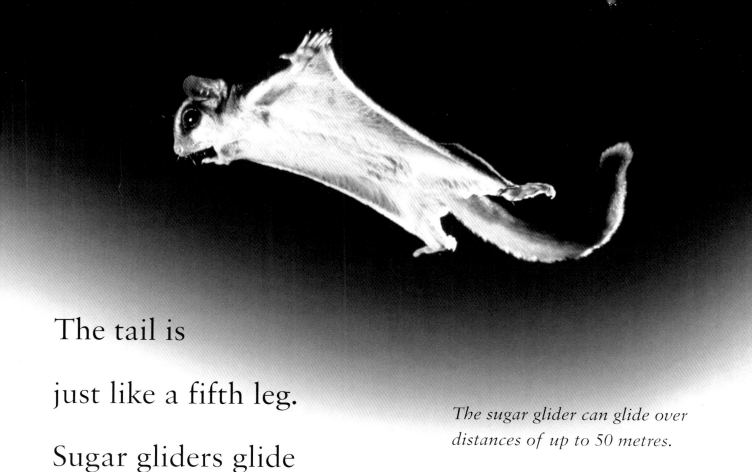

The tail is

just like a fifth leg.

The sugar glider can glide over distances of up to 50 metres.

Sugar gliders glide

between trees. They have a flap of skin between

their arms and legs that

acts like a wing. This flap

helps to keep the sugar

glider in the air.

A brush-tailed possum uses its long tail to grip a piece of wood as it feeds.

19

Coming out at night

Nocturnal marsupials sleep during the day and come out at night to feed. It is safer to feed at night because **predators** cannot see them.

This small, mouse-like antechinus comes out at night to hunt insects, worms and spiders.

The brush-tailed possum is a night-time visitor to gardens and parks.

If they came out during the day they could be spotted and eaten. Desert marsupials hide during the day to escape the heat of the sun. They come out at night because it is cooler.

The long-nosed bandicoot leaves cone-shaped holes in the ground as it hunts for insects at night.

Digging burrows

Some marsupials dig **burrows** and tunnels in the ground. They use them to hide in and to build their nests. The wombat has long claws, which it uses to dig through the soil.

The strong claws of the wombat are perfect for digging through soil.

The wombats' teeth are suited to chewing on tough grasses and roots.

They dig out a network of tunnels with lots of entrances. The marsupial mole has hands with extra large, flat claws. It burrows through the soil to find food, but any tunnels the marsupial mole builds soon collapse.

The bilby builds a burrow that is about three metres long and two metres deep.

Baby marsupials

Marsupials give birth to tiny babies that crawl into their mother's pouch to feed on their mother's milk. They gradually get bigger until they fill the pouch.

A tiny brush-tailed possum sucks on its mothers teat to get milk while it is in the pouch.

Young Virginia opossums leave their mother's pouch when they are about 70 days old.

The babies may stay in

the pouch for several months until they are

large enough to

feed themselves.

Once a young koala reaches six months of age it is carried around on its mother's back.

Big relatives

The largest marsupials are the kangaroos.
The red kangaroo stands up to 160 cm high
and has a tail that is one metre long. It bounds
along at speeds of up to 55 mph and each leap is
long enough to clear two cars.

*The red kangaroo is
the largest marsupial.*

A kangaroo bounds across the ground using its long hind legs.

Kangaroos give birth to a single baby called a **joey**. The joey may spend six months in its mother's pouch.

A female Eastern grey kangaroo and her joey.

Investigate!

Living in the garden

People who live in North America and Australia may be lucky enough to have marsupials living in their gardens. If you have marsupials in your garden you can watch them to see what they eat and how they move. In other parts of the world, marsupials can be seen in zoos and wildlife parks.

Watch how a marsupial moves around in a zoo, wildlife park or in your garden.

Pouches

You could pretend to have a pouch and see what it feels like to carry a young marsupial around. Tie a large apron around your waist and place a stuffed toy in the pocket. Imagine what it would be like to be a marsupial with a pouch full of wriggling babies! How easy is it for you to move around?

See what it feels like to carry a baby around in a pouch.

Hops and leaps

Many marsupials have long back legs and get around by hopping and leaping. See how far you can hop with your feet together. Can you hop further if you hop on one leg?

Place your feet together and try bounding like a kangaroo. How far can you leap with your feet together?

Find out about marsupials

You can learn more about marsupials by visiting a local library to read books on marsupials. You can also search for information on the Internet.

Marsupial facts

✓ The quokka was one of the first marsupials seen by Europeans when they arrived in Australia. They thought it was a rat.

✓ The musky rat-kangaroo is the only kangaroo that gives birth to twins.

✓ The yapok or water opossum swims and is the only marsupial with **webbed** feet.

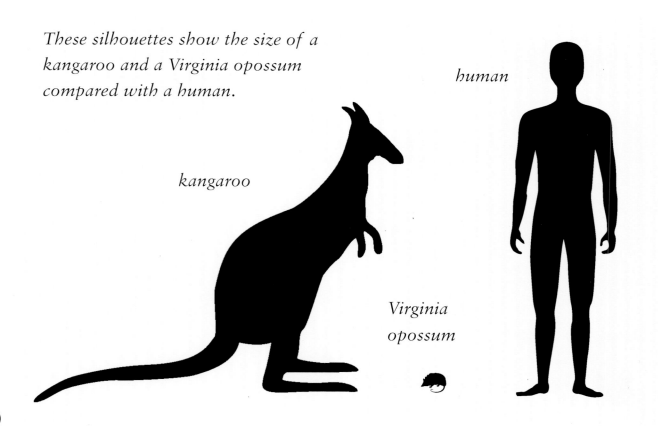

These silhouettes show the size of a kangaroo and a Virginia opossum compared with a human.

human

kangaroo

Virginia opossum

Glossary

burrow large hole or tunnel in the ground.

carnivore an animal that eats other animals.

herbivore an animal that only eats plants.

joey the name given to the young of a kangaroo.

mammal an animal that feeds their young with milk and is covered in fur.

marsupial a mammal that has a pouch.

nectar the sugary liquid produced by certain flowers.

nocturnal active at night, sleeps during the day.

pouch a small pocket or flap of skin on the tummy of a female marsupial.

predators animals that hunt and eat other animals for food.

prey an animal that is hunted by other animals.

webbed having flaps of skin between the toes.

Index